MW00907598

ISBN: Softcover 978-1-5434-6037-7
Hardcover 978-1-5434-6036-0
EBook 978-1-5434-6038-4

Print information available on the last page

Rev. date: 11/15/2017

To order additional copies of this book, contact:
Xlibris
1-888-795-4274
www.Xlibris.com
Orders@Xlibris.com

Four Legged Heroes©

THE Mama Magina Books

A trio of true stories about courage, determination, and fortitude. Includes vocabulary and character building exercise.

Author
Mary Virginia McCormick Pittman©

Book Design & Illustration
by Carol A. Howell©

To Leah Virginia . . .
My "Precious Package",
Who makes "My Magic"
Happen!
Your Mama Magina

Table of Contents

The heroic and noble Siberian Husky **Lead** sled–dog, who led his "musher" and indomitable sled–dog team through the extraordinary, sub-zero, treacherous, Alaskan wilderness to the village of Nome, to save the children from the insidious, epidemic, disease, Diphtheria, in 1925!

All Bush planes were grounded, all ships iced-in, and all trains were trapped by huge snow banks. The only chance of getting the precious vaccine through was by Relay sled-dog teams . . .

A huge majestic statue of **Balto** currently stands in Central Park of New York City to honor him, and the unique DNA instinct, grit, and ultimate determination of descendants of the Wolf!

The Plight of the Polar Bear

On one of my early trips of many, to the Arctic and Sub-Arctic, to do research and gather data on the plight of the Polar Bear and the effects of Global Warming, sometimes, it was necessary to utilize Sled-Dogs and "mush" over the snow and ice. Having learned to "mush Huskies" in the snow covered San Jacinto Mountains, high above the Palm Springs Desert, in California, when I was younger, it was sheer pleasure for me to re-live my "mushing days", now, in the Sub-zero weather of the Sub-Arctic. I love the Sled Dogs; Huskies, Alaskan Malamute, Indian Dogs, Russian Siberian Samoyed, and sometimes a hybrid Wolf. They are affectionate, loyal, protective, and they *love* to run . . . their stamina and zeal are to be justifiably admired.

On the day I was to select my "mushing" team of dogs, the owner-handler insisted that he had a "special" lead-dog for me . . . "Tiffany", a beautiful, half-wolf and half-Husky dog, with six weaned pups. Our connection was immediate! She wagged her tail vigorously and enjoyed my scratching her ears and talking baby-talk to her. She looked into my eyes, studying me intensely, with her kind brown eyes.

The following morning, I was greeted with paws upon my shoulders and kisses upon my face.

Tiffany was ready to "run" with me! The owner of these dogs said that he had never seen her act this way with anyone before! Harnessing sled-dogs is a "celebration" . . . excitement and yips abound. The dogs are impatient. They cannot wait to do what they were created to do.

It is important for your team to know you, as their "musher", and to sense who you are and what to expect from you. On the trail, it is only the "musher" and team ... in an unpredictable environment! A six foot long, ship-mooring cable, dangles off the back of the sled. Should a musher fall from the ski-rungs of the sled, that saving cable can be quickly grabbed. Otherwise, the dogs will be far down the trail, and a musher alone in severe weather, in a wilderness, with wild animals, can immediately be in serious danger. I stepped upon the sled ski-rungs, and pulled the anchor-stake of the sled. All were anticipating that "magic word", "Hike"! And we were off like a bullet ... Invigorating ... You feel free!

That day we were "making trail"! That means working our way through deep, freshly fallen snow, that has not been packed down by other sleds before us. Non-mushers think that all a musher does is to take a ride on the ski-rungs of a sled, pulled by dogs. It could not be further from the truth!

A musher works with the dogs, the entire "run"; encouraging the dogs, praising them, and stepping one foot off the rung of the sled in order to help push the sled on up-hill knolls and rough terrain. The "wheel dogs" mostly pull the weight of the sled, so they must have strong hind-quarters.

A helpful push from the musher helps to save the strength of the dogs.

Sometimes two dogs may start to squabble in their traces, while on the trail. Then, you shout-out, not harshly, but strongly, "cut it out, boys and girls!". They obey! Your voice is their command. Sometimes I would sing to them and other times we would simply enjoy the pleasure of the rhythm of our pace and the silence and appreciation of our surroundings and our togetherness. There is a peace within.

There is a spectacular partnership and a relationship with the musher and the dogs. Our lives depend upon each other in sometimes hostile situations. We move along, making good time, when, suddenly, Tiffany stops the team. "Hike, Tiffany", I say. She does not move. I drive the anchor-stake into the ground, step off the ski-rungs, and pick up my prod pole from the sled, as I slog through the snow almost up to my knees. She turns her head towards me and waits patiently. As I approach, she wags her tail in greeting. "What's the matter, Ol' girl", I ask, as I pet her head. She looks straight ahead. My eyes follow her direction. So I step forward two feet and jab the prod pole through the snow. Beyond the snow, solid ground. Tiffany continues to look forward a little distance. So I step forward a little more cautiously. And jab my pole again. I hear ice crack below the snow. I look at Tiffany! I bend down and hug her. "You've probably saved us, Ol' Girl"! The other dogs now, know something is not right. They are actually quiet! "OK", I say to Tiffany. "Take us where you want us to go"! I slog back to the sled, grateful! "The wolf in her has surely saved us", I knew! At the sled I replaced the prod pole, and picked up a long thin aluminum pole with an orange flag attached. I put it to the side of our trail, deep in the snow, to warn other mushers of the potential danger, might they come our way. I boarded my ski-rungs, pulled the anchor-stake, and shouted, "Hike"! Tiffany made a hard "Gee" (to the right) with the team, and we were off again.

We were reaching the bay, a new area now, so I searched for a sheltered place to protect us from a rising wind. I found one against a snow and ice embankment. It was time for food and a short rest for the dogs. Staying in their traces, I fed the dogs, a small meal for now. Their big meal would be at the end of our trip, for the day. As I fed, I petted each one. When I got to Tiffany, I gave a royal hug! They then hunkered down in the snow for warmth and took their short nap. I quickly provided my own provisions. Protein is most important! I had brought a small steak and made a small fire with a camp oven... Eating the meat as soon as it was chewable, otherwise it would rapidly freeze.

Within the hour we were off mushing at a good pace. The snow was more packed and there was more horizon as we neared the waters of the bay ... looking for Polar Bears, hungrily marauding the shores, waiting for the water to freeze and become sea ice; impatiently. They needed to go hunting for their favorite food, the seals!

Polar Bears

dine on fat, not meat, and seals are nature's chosen menu.

Now that I could see in the distance, I studied the horizon carefully and intently ... Yes, there in the distance, I could see Polar Bears. I stopped the sled team with a "Whoa"! The dogs stood still but yipping. I took my binoculars but stayed on the ski-rungs of the sled. I counted only twelve Polar Bears, rather close together, cavorting, play-fighting, and watching the water. One bear even entered the water to test the chill. Polar Bears are a curious lot with excellent eye sight, hearing, and a keen sense of smell. They have no predator but mankind. However, although they certainly are not afraid of the dogs or any other animal, they do not appreciate a team of noisy, yipping dogs. So they prefer to stay away.

Satisfied with my accurate account of only a dozen bears, for the day, and with the good health of the bears, in spite of some weight loss, I spoke to my team, "Hike"! "We're on our way home now"... I shouted out!

After an eight hour day, on the trail, we arrived at camp. I helped to unharness my dogs. With each dog I gave a certain treat that I always bring with me – two large pieces each of real beef jerky from Oak Ridge Farms, Texas.

And, I am the only musher who does that! In the snow, I walked Tiffany back to her large kennel house where her pups, were waiting. I squatted down, in order to hug her neck, and scratch her ears, and thank her again for a safe day. She vigorously reciprocated – with her wagging tail, kisses and nuzzles. I then said, "I have to go now"! She was startled and looked at me with serious concern. I immediately realized that she thought I was "going away". "Oh, no", I said. "I will see you tomorrow ", assuring her. She brightened but looked at me questionably ...

I quickly responded, with a little laugh, as I reached out to hug her again, "Yes, Tiffany, I will see you tomorrow, for sure"! She wagged her tail, satisfied, and nuzzled me one more time and scampered off to her pups. I watched her a few more moments as she greeted her young with joyful enthusiasm, and then licked and checked out each pup individually ... the wonderment of her motherhood!

I arose and walked to our base camp house, looking forward to a nice warm bath and a hot meal, beside a cozy fireplace. With a big smile, I said to myself, "Yes, Tiffany, I *will* see you tomorrow, for sure!"

The Iditarod Trail Sled-Dog "Race Of Mercy," 1925

The Iditarod Trail Sled-Dog Race, every year in March, ceremoniously honors the miraculous true story from 1925, of a Siberian Husky, "Lead" Sled-dog, Balto. Balto, with his "musher," and sled-dog team, including other sled-dog Relay Teams, who traveled against valuable time, the 647 miles from Nenana to Nome, Alaska ... Enduring the most severe, sub-zero cold of the Alaskan wilderness, with blizzards, "white-outs', and the treacherous frozen Bering Sea Coast terrain. This was undertaken to deliver the precious vaccine, and save the lives of the Nome Village, and its sick children from the insidious, killer disease, Diphtheria! Balto and the *Relay Teams* made it through due to the unique DNA instinct and their determination, which is The Spirit of the Wolf!

A huge, magnificent statue, honoring Balto, and symbolizing his fellow sled-dog teams, stands mounted in Central Park in New York City today!

On January 20th, 1925, the call went out from doctors in Nome, an isolated town in Alaska, close to the Bering Sea Coast, the insidious killer disease, Diphtheria had hit! Antitoxin vaccine was desperately needed!

Coffins were already being built ... Bush planes were grounded, ships were iced-in, and trains were trapped by huge banks of snow. Sled-dogs were the only chance to get the antitoxin vaccine through to Nome in time!

A train carrying the precious vaccine took 2 days from Anchorage to the rail head at Nenana. From Nenana to Nome it would have to be by sled dogs along the Iditarod Trail.

A normal travel time of 25 days, over 647 miles! Relay Teams-Pony Express style, were quickly arranged. 20 "mushers" and 150 dogs answered the call.

On January 25th, the 1st team departed from Nenana. "The Great Race of Mercy" was on, carrying the precious cargo!

As the team departed, a horrific, "blinding white-out" blizzard, covering the territory set-in!

The storm was moving in, with temperatures dropping -40 degrees to -50 degrees below-Fahrenheit, with gusts of wind up to 50 miles an hour and more, that would sometimes turn over or lift the sleds and dogs up and off the ground.

Togo, the incredible, brave, leader of the second-to-last team, racing to Nome, covered 200 miles and courageously transversed across the perilous Norton Sound – saving his team and musher while swimming through the ice floes.

The Final Leg Hand-off, in the village of Bluff, was to Balto, a Siberian Husky, *lead sled-dog,* with his "musher," Gunnar Kassen. The heroic Balto's spirit was up to the overwhelming challenge of the cruel weather, in spite of the winds lifting his sled and his valiant team of dogs up high into the air! Balto stayed on his course, even when his musher, Kassen, found himself unable to navigate the sled, and began to hold almost no hope of making it to Nome.

Balto took charge, following his instincts, and with his indominatable team, fought on through the terrain of the most treacherous Bering Sea Cost Territory. Over 20 hours ... and, mostly in the dark!

At dawn, 5:30 A.M., February 2, 1925, Balto and his courageous team of sled dogs and musher "charged into the remote village of Nome, Alaska!" The antitoxin vaccine *was* delivered! "The dogs were so spent, they could not even bark!" But they were happy! The joyous excitement of the people told them something extraordinary had happened!

The remote village of Nome and its' children were saved!!

The 647 miles, from Nenana, were traversed in 5-1/2 days and 127-1/2 hours – during one of Alaska's fiercest winters, the "impossible" had become an unfathomable "Miracle!"

From the beginning, multiple hearts, minds, hands, and paws, had answered the call to a historical event that seemed to be destined to failure. During one of Alaska's most wicked winters, and in spite of unthinkable odds against them, *600 paws*, of Four-Legged Heroes gave their all . . . their strength, zeal, stamina, courage, bravery, and unstoppable determination, to make a miracle to save mankind!

A normal 25 days to traverse the distance . . . the 647 miles was made in an unimaginably swift, 5-1/2 days, 127-1/2 hours, in the severe cold and "white-out" blizzard, and treacherous winds of one of Alaska's most brutal winters"!

One of the **greatest** *rescues in American History ...*
by the descendants of the Wolf!

This year in March, 2017, 2,000 dogs belonging to 72 "mushers", from around the world, gathered in Anchorage, Alaska, for the race. The ceremonial start is fan-friendly, to show-off "mushing" to fans. Spectators pet the dogs, mingle with the mushers and grab an autograph or two. People lucky enough to win auctions for a prime spot in a competitors sled, travel over an 11 mile course on city trails and streets. Anchorage, Alaska's largest city, is in a full party mode all the way out of town! "Seeing the personal interaction between the "mushers" and their dogs is just spectacular"..."Everybody should see it once!"

This year, a 30 year old "musher" Dallas Seavey, won his 4th, out of the last five, Iditarod races! (API) March 5, 2017.

Headquarters for The Iditarod Trail Sled-Dog Race

"The Last Great Race on Earth", is in Wasilla, Alaska. Named after Chief Wasilla of the local Dena'ina Athabaskan Tribe, Wasilla was formerly a mining supply station. Today, it is a fast-paced City of nearly 10,000 population, and has become an out-door activity paradise, surrounded by lakes, rivers, and majestic mountains!

For more information, please use the following numbers and links:

iditarod.com/resources/about/contact-iditarod-staff/

Phone: (907) 376-5155 x104 ... For a list of FAQ's visit this link: http://info.iditarod.com/. Iditarod Trail ...

Phone Room: (907) 248-MUSH (6874) RACE TIME ONLY!

Mama Magina and Leah "mush huskies" . . .

From the first time Mama Magina told stories to her precious granddaughter, Leah Virginia, about her conservation and humanitarian trips, to help save animals and people in other countries, Leah wanted to know everything that Mama Magina did on those trips. And, Leah said that she wanted to grow up and do the same thing!

Then Leah wanted to learn how to take those adventures and turn them into something that she and her grandmother could play.

And that is how the game "Mushing Huskies" was born!

Each night just before bedtime, Leah would bring a number of her plush animals to the sleigh-bed in her pink bedroom, and place them like sled dogs in harness on the bed. Mama Magina would be in the bed and Leah would put herself beside Mama Magina, pretending to be in another sled. That meant twelve (12,) "stuffed", plush animals at one time – six for each pretend sled.

With their backs in front of the bed-pillows with legs stretched out to be the sleds, and plush animals "dogs" in pretend harness, two-by-two- by two, for pulling their pretend sleds, . . . *They* were ready to go! The only thing available for the harness and leads, was bright, pink, ribbon!

Mama Magina taught Leah how the "musher" must pull the anchor-stake from the ground before the famous words, "Hike!" ... or "Mush!", to command the dogs to "run"! And "run" they do! These sled-dogs are bred to "run" and they love to do it!

"We bounce a little on the bed to signify the movements of our sleds. Our imaginations rule the rest of our sled adventure. We see moose sometimes crossing our trail ahead. We see rabbits scampering across the snow, leaving their foot prints. Sometimes a large tree branch falls from a fir tree along our trail, because of the heaviness of the snow on its branches. The sub-zero temperature is quite biting and cold, but, we are "dressed" for such severe weather, with our pretend "Mustang Suits", which protects our bodies from freezing!

Sometimes we have to "make trail"! That means mushing through freshly fallen, and deep snow where other dog-sled teams have not passed by and packed down the trail of snow! That is harder work for the dogs, so many times a musher will step one foot off the rung of the sled and help to push the sled to save the energy of the dogs.

We are reaching the bay area about now, so we search for a sheltered place to protect us from the rising winds.

We find one against a snow and ice embankment. It is time for food and a short rest for the dogs. Staying in their traces, we feed our dogs, a small meal for now. Their big meal will come at the end of our trip for the day. As we feed the dogs, we pat each one. They then hunker down in the snow for warmth and take a short nap.

We quickly provide our own provisions. Protein is most important! We brought two small steaks and make a fire with our camp oven . . . eating our meat as soon as it is thawed, otherwise it would rapidly freeze.

Dogs and mushers have a very special relationship: So we talk to our dogs, praise and encourage them, and sometimes, sing to them. And, sometimes we just enjoy the silence in our surroundings, with only the small sounds of the sled sliding through the ice and snow. Sometimes, we pretend to hear wolves howling in the distance . . .

(Of course, we have studied maps and the animals that we might actually see on a real sled dog run.)

"This makes learning fun Mama Magina", said Leah!

Often, we decide to take food with us, on the sled, to throw out on the snow for animals in a really harsh winter . . . Hay for moose and protein pellets for the rabbits, and more. Now and then, we take meat for a stray wolf lost from its pack.

Suddenly, Mommie opens the bedroom door and sings out, "Bedtime" . . . and, we respond, "Five minutes"! "We are on our way to camp"!

So we head toward camp with a "Gee" (to the right) and, when we come to another turn, on our trail, we shout, "Haw" (to the left), and, the dogs know now we are headed home . . . When we arrive at camp, we say, "Whoa", and put down our anchor-stake into the ground.

Then, we unharness our dogs, talking to and petting each one, giving them their nightly meal, and taking them to their kennel which is Leah's old crib, when she was a baby!

We've had a really good day "mushing"! In bed, we say our prayers, and "hugs", and turn off the light with a "Where was Moses when the lights went out"? Leah shouts out, "In the dark"! (That said "in fun" helps children to be unafraid of the dark. Said *every* night, children feel the "dark" is friendly for sleep ...)

We've had a really good adventurous day, "Mushing"!"

And, so can you! Good Night, and sweet "Mushing" dreams, from Mama Magina, and Leah.

The End

What is the Spirit of the Wolf?

The wolf represents the symbol to mankind of courage, faithfulness, vigilance, loyalty, strength, and perseverance. The magnificent *Balto*, is the embodiment of these traits.

Have you ever felt yourself attracted to the wolf, and enjoyed the sound of it's lonely howl in the moonlight? Was it calling to you from the mountain top? Perhaps you have the *spirit of the wolf* deep within you?

Ancient peoples consider the wolf to be mysterious, majestic and wise.
Wolf spirit is trusting, loyal, courageous, and teaches us to be true to ourselves and follow our unique purpose in life. To have the wolf spirit is to be lonely at times, forever vigilant, caring for the pack, sharing in the hard times as well as the times of great bounty. The wolf's attachment to one another is firm and committed, lasting, and true. The wolf teaches us to trust our own hearts and minds, staying true to our innermost intentions.

Wolves howl for themselves as well as to signal other wolves. A pack may travel 40-50 kilometers a day, or 30 - 40 miles. The average wolf pack consists of 5 to 8 wolves, but can be as many as 30. Wolves run on their toes which enables them to turn quickly, and prevents their paws from wearing down.

A true story of the wolf's survival instinct, tells of an arctic wolf pack, together digging a 15 foot deep den to escape the heat and smoke as a wildfire raged overhead ...
They Survived!

The wolf, a symbol of the night, may be seen as frightening. So frightening in fact that the ancient Vikings wore wolf skins to war to invoke their powerful spirits and give the warriors strength and vitality for battle. However, Native Americans see the wolf as teachers and pathfinders that will lead us to our innermost self. When the wolf spirit enters our life it will bring faithfulness, inner strength, and sharpen our intuition. Most importantly, the wolf teaches us to trust our intuition.

The Genetic Science Research community over decades of research have proven that all breeds of dog have evolved from the unique genetic DNA of the Wolf.

Be Who You Were Meant to Be

You can remove this worksheet page by gently tearing, using the perforation, and use it to create a character building notebook for your child.

How to use the "Spirit of the Wolf" discussion worksheet.

1. Discuss the chosen trait with your child. Have them look up the word in a dictionary, not using a computer.

2. Ask them, "What does courage mean to you?"
(After they have an idea formulated, have them write it in the space provided.)

3. Next, ask the child what color they envision this trait to be?
(Explain that "traits" do not actually have a color, but ask them to pretend that it does.)

4. Color the circle provided with the preferred color.
(For example, if the child says, "I think courage is blue!" They should proceed to color in the circle with a blue colored pencil or crayon.)

5. Ask the child to think about an experience they had when they saw someone being courageous, or they themselves behaved in a a courageous way.
Have them print that personal experience in the space provided.

6. When they are finished, ask them to read their story out loud, and then close their eyes and envision the color they selected for that trait.

7. Proceed this way through all 6 traits and then celebrate the fact that they now possess the "Spirit of the Wolf." Please color the wolf provided by Freepik.com when you are done with the exercise.

These steps may be repeated once or twice a week, and also used as a game, to thoroughly imbed these positive traits.

C - F - V - L - S - P - A mnemonic to help you memorize these desireable wolf traits.

1. How can you be **Courageous?**

2. What does it mean to be **Faithful?**

3. Have you ever been **Vigilant?**

4. What might test your **Loyalty?**

5. How can you develop Inner **Strength?**

6. What does **Perservance** mean?

Art courtesy of Freepik.com

Dog-Sled "Speak"

Alaskan husky: a northern dog of mixed breed, usually used to denote those bred for racing.
Basket: the main body of a sled, where passengers or gear may be carried.
Booties: slippers for dogs, worn while working under certain conditions to prevent ice forming between their toes. Made of a wide range of fabrics, including fleece and Gore-tex
Brushbow: the curved piece out in front of the main body of a sled, designed to stop brush from damaging the sled.
Dog Bag: a fabric bag carried on a race sled, used to put a sick or injured dog into in order to carry him to a place where he can be cared for.
Dog Box: a carrier for several dogs, most often seen as a wooden structure in the bed of a pickup truck. Styles vary widely, but usually built with individual sections that hold one or two dogs each.
Driving Bow: the handle that the musher holds on to - also called a Handlebow.
Easy!: the command for the dogs to slow down.
Gangline: the main line that the dogs and sled are attached to.
Gee - the command for the dogs to turn right.
Handler - a person who assists the musher.
Harness: a webbing of fabric that fits a dog snugly, to which the Tugline and Neckline are attached.
Haw - the command for the dogs to turn left.
Hike! - the command to get the dog team moving.
Husky - in common useage, any northern breed dog - properly, a Siberian Husky.
Lead Dogs: the dog or dogs in the front of a team. These dogs are noted for their high level of intelligence and drive, and are often females. May be run as Single lead (1 dog) or Double lead (2 dogs).
Mush!: many people think this is the term used to get a team going - Hike! is most commonly used.
Musher: a person who drives a sled dog team - also called a Dog Driver.

Neckline: a short line (10-12 inches) attached to the Harness and Gangline, that keeps the dog in line.
On By!: the command to go by another team or other distraction.
Pedaling: pushing with one foot while keeping the other on the sled.
Point Dogs - used by some mushers to denote the two dogs right behind the Lead Dogs. Others call them Swing Dogs.
Rigging: all the gear used to attach dogs to a sled.
Runners: the narrow pieces of wood that a sled rides on. Usually have a replaceable plastic layer to reduce maintenance. The runners extend behind the Basket so the Musher can stand on them.
Safety Line: an extra line from the Gangline to the sled, in case the main fitting breaks.
Snow Hook: a large metal hook that can be driven into firm snow to anchor a team for a short period of time without tying them.
Snub Line: a rope attached to the back of the sled, which can be tied to a tree to hold the team when the snow is not firm enough to use a Snow Hook.
Stakeout: a main chain with separate short chains to attach several dogs to. May be strung between the front and back bumpers of a truck, or between two trees.
Stanchions: the upright pieces that attach the runners to a sled.
Swing Dogs: depending on which musher you're talking to, either the two dogs directly behind the Lead Dogs, or those between the Point Dogs and the Wheel Dogs.
Tack: harnesses
Team Dogs: all dogs other than the Lead Dogs, Point Dogs, Swing Dogs and Wheel Dogs.
Toboggan: a sled with a flat bottom instead of runners. Used when deep, soft snow is expected instead of a good trail.
Tuglines: the main line that connects the dog's harness to the Gangline - the line that the dog tugs on.
Village Dogs: a derogatory term for poorly socialized dogs of unknown origin

Mushing Vocabulary from White Mountain Shoes:
http://www.everythinghusky.com/features/mushingterms.html

My Gratitude and Appreciation

To my dear Carol A. Howell for sharing her talent and genius, to Reyna Lace and Dana Scott, for their guidance and professionalism,
and to Judy Gale S., Derek "Blazer" C., Commander R. Glenn L., Don Wayne B., Jan and Bob S., Evelyn and Ray H., Col. Paul B., Sydney and Ted R., Geo. Ben J., Sandra T., and Jan Price L., for their abiding love, trust and friendship to me through my journey in life!

Mary Virginia McCormick Pittman

CPSIA information can be obtained at www.ICGtesting.com
Printed in the USA
LVIW01n2243071217
559040LV00004B/17